What Was
the First Thanksgiving?

by Joan Holub

illustrated by Lauren Mortimer

Grosset & Dunlap
An Imprint of Penguin Group (USA)

For Debbie Randolph and Jay Gallagher, with
thanks for the Thanksgivings at their house—JH

GROSSET & DUNLAP
Published by the Penguin Group
Penguin Group (USA), 375 Hudson Street, New York, New York 10014, USA

USA | Canada | UK | Ireland | Australia | New Zealand | India | South Africa | China
Penguin Books Ltd, Registered Offices: 80 Strand, London WC2R 0RL, England

For more information about the Penguin Group visit penguin.com

Text copyright © 2013 by Joan Holub. Illustrations copyright © 2013 by
Penguin Group (USA). All rights reserved. Published by Grosset & Dunlap, a division
of Penguin Young Readers Group, 345 Hudson Street, New York, New York 10014.
GROSSET & DUNLAP is a trademark of Penguin Group (USA). Printed in the U.S.A.

Library of Congress Cataloging-in-Publication Data is available.

ISBN 978-0-448-46463-3   10 9 8

Contents

What Was the First Thanksgiving? 1

Puritans 5

Sailing to America 12

Land! 22

A New Home 28

Making Friends 40

The First Thanksgiving 54

Fun and Games 64

Trouble 70

A Thanksgiving Holiday 78

Thanksgiving Today 86

Timelines 102

Bibliography 104

What Was the First Thanksgiving?

The first Thanksgiving was a feast to celebrate the Pilgrims' first harvest. It took place in Plymouth, Massachusetts, in 1621. And it lasted for three whole days. There was a lot of eating. There were probably games. There were more Native American guests than Pilgrims. It was a happy time.

The Pilgrims had sailed to America from England in 1620. They came on a ship named the *Mayflower*.

What exactly is a pilgrim?

A pilgrim is someone who goes on a long trip in God's name. The Pilgrims on the *Mayflower* traveled all the way across the Atlantic Ocean to find religious freedom. They wanted to worship God in their own way.

That first summer in America, the corn grew strong and tall. Beans, squash, and pumpkins grew in the fields. Carrots, turnips, and onions grew in the gardens by their homes. In the fall, it was time to harvest. There would be plenty to eat in the coming winter. So the Pilgrims wanted to give thanks. And they did.

Today Thanksgiving is a national holiday in the United States. It falls on the fourth Thursday of November. It's a day to be thankful for many things, including having enough to eat. It's a day for sharing. Families and friends get together. They play football games or see them on TV. They watch parades.

The first Thanksgiving happened so long ago. Some facts are not certain. No one is sure if the

Pilgrims actually invited the Native Americans to their Thanksgiving feast. Perhaps the natives heard the Pilgrims shooting their muskets and went to investigate, bringing weapons in case of trouble. So it could have turned into a fight that long-ago day instead of a wonderful three-day party!

CHAPTER 1
Puritans

In the early 1600s, King James I ruled England. He made the laws and ran the government. Everyone had to be Christian and join the Church of England. No one could choose a different religion. Whatever rules the king made, everyone had to obey them. Or else.

King James I

Some people called themselves Puritans. They were Christians. But they didn't want to be part of the Church of England. They believed the Bible was the law in religion. Not the king. Some Puritans wanted to separate from the king's church. They started their own churches and held prayer meetings. They had to do it in secret. Otherwise King James could have thrown them in jail!

Some Puritans escaped to Holland in 1608. In Holland they were free to worship the way they liked. They stayed for twelve years. But it was hard to get good-paying jobs in Holland. And they felt out of place. They were English, but now their children were speaking Dutch, the language of Holland. They wanted a place they could call their own. They decided to travel to the New World. That was what people in Europe called North America back then.

The Puritans worked out a deal with a company. They got a ship, a crew, and some cargo. As soon as they were settled in the New World, the Puritans would get to work. They would cut trees and go hunting and fishing. They'd send lumber, furs, and fish back to England. They would pay back the company and eventually own the land they had settled.

Not all of the Puritans in Holland were going to be able to make the trip. That was okay with some. They were too scared to go. They were afraid the ship might sink. And there were stories about natives attacking English settlements.

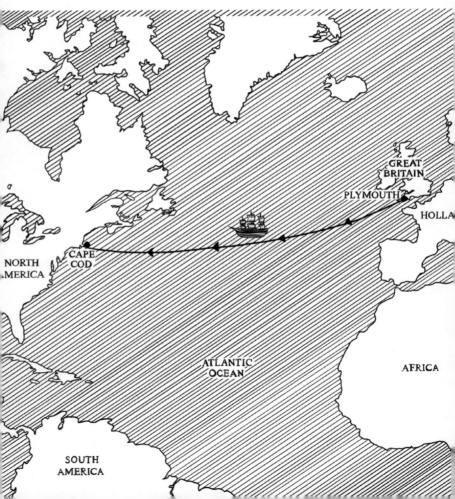

But around forty-five Puritans would soon sail across an ocean in a small ship for a chance at a new life in the New World.

Jamestown, the First English Colony

In December 1606, three ships from England set sail to the New World. Together, they carried 104 settlers, all men and boys. They arrived in Virginia in April 1607. On May 13, they chose a spot along the James River and began building a fort. Their settlement was called Jamestown, in honor of King James.

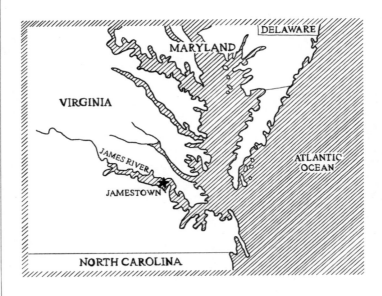

Native American Algonquians already had been living in Virginia for hundreds of years. They were led by the powerful Chief Powhatan. For a while, the tribe traded with the colonists. But the colonists were taking over their land. The tribe began attacking the settlers. In the winter of 1610, they surrounded the colony. Trapped, the colonists were soon starving. Only sixty settlers survived.

Chief Powhatan

Jamestown was the first permanent English colony in North America. It doesn't exist anymore. However, you can visit historic Jamestown in Williamsburg, Virginia. There's a re-created fort, a Native American village, and actual-size models of the three ships that brought the English colonists to Virginia.

CHAPTER 2
Sailing to America

In Holland, the Puritans bought a small ship called the *Speedwell*. On July 22, 1620, they sailed to Southampton, England, where they met up with a second ship called the *Mayflower*.

On August 15, the two ships headed for the New World. Almost right away, the *Speedwell* started to leak. It was in no shape to cross an ocean.

The *Speedwell*

The *Mayflower*

That left only one ship—the *Mayflower*. It was 106 feet long and 25 feet wide. That's about three-quarters as long as a high-school basketball court and only half as wide. But it was the *Mayflower* or nothing.

Not all of the Puritans from the *Speedwell* would fit on the *Mayflower*. In all, the *Mayflower* ended up carrying 102 passengers. There were thirty-two children, fifty men, and twenty women. Some of them were servants.

Was everyone a Puritan?

No.

About half were. Other passengers were simply looking for a better life in the New World. But today we call all 102 *Mayflower* passengers "Pilgrims."

Besides the passengers, there were about twenty-five sailors. One of them was a doctor. He would care for lots of seasick patients. The Puritans also invited along a soldier named Captain Myles Standish to protect them in the New World. Two dogs came—a mastiff and a springer spaniel. There were probably chickens, goats, pigs, and cats, too.

On September 6, 1620, the *Mayflower* set sail.

Captain Myles Standish

Nothing about the trip was easy. The ship should have left sooner, in the summer. Now it was fall. Winter was coming and would bring bad weather.

The Atlantic Ocean was calm at first. But about halfway across, terrible storms hit. Enormous waves bounced the *Mayflower* up and down, up and down. The Pilgrims feared they would die. Many got seasick and threw up.

Most of the time they hid from the storm in a dark, cramped part of the ship. It was meant for storing cargo and was only about five feet high. The Pilgrims couldn't even stand up straight. Only a lucky few had beds. Most slept in hammocks or on the floor.

Like many people in the 1600s, the Pilgrims thought taking a bath could give you a cold. They didn't bathe very often. So the ship got really smelly after a while. People got bitten by fleas, and got lice, too.

Because of the delay in starting out, much of the food had been eaten. There wasn't enough fresh water, either. Rats got into everything. Cheese got moldy. Day after day, the menu was dried peas, dried codfish, salted pork or beef, and hard bread.

There wasn't much privacy. People could hear everything you said. There were no bathrooms. The Pilgrims used buckets called chamber pots for toilets. Full chamber pots got emptied overboard.

There was a lot of arguing. The Puritans tried to boss around everyone who wasn't a Puritan. The ship's crew teased the Puritans for praying so much and for the way they spoke. For instance, they said "thee" instead of "you."

Just when it seemed things couldn't get worse, there was another big storm. One of the *Mayflower*'s main beams cracked. The captain wanted to return to England. But the Puritans were not going to do that. They repaired the ship's beam. The *Mayflower* sailed on.

The *Mayflower II*

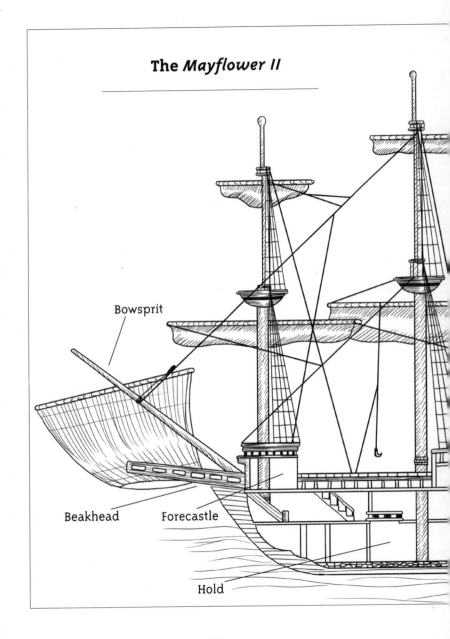

Bowsprit

Beakhead

Forecastle

Hold

You can go aboard an actual-size ship called the *Mayflower II*. It's an almost-exact copy of the original *Mayflower*. It was built in England in 1957 and sailed to America.

On the ship, you may meet people pretending to be sailors or passengers on the *Mayflower* in 1620. They will tell you what it was like to sail to America. The *Mayflower II* is docked at Pilgrim Memorial State Park in downtown Plymouth, Massachusetts.

Roundhouse

Captain's cabin

Whipstaff

Steerage room

Tiller

Gun room

Tween deck

CHAPTER 3
Land!

Finally, on November 9, 1620, land was spotted. The *Mayflower* had been on the ocean for sixty-five days. One sailor and one servant boy had gotten sick and died. One baby had been born. He was named Oceanus because he was born while crossing the Atlantic.

Imagine how glad the Pilgrims were. They had made it to the New World!

But there was one big problem. They weren't where they were supposed to be. The storms had blown them too far north. Instead of New York, they were at Cape Cod, Massachusetts!

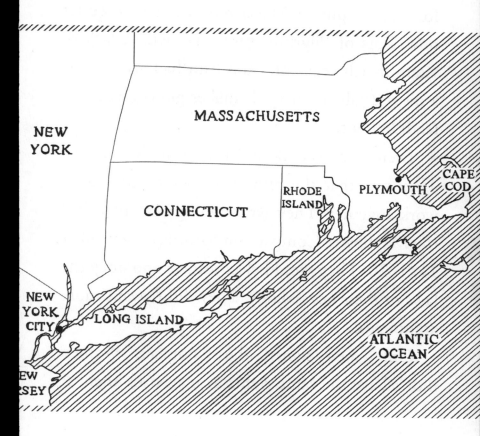

Still, they were so happy that they had survived the trip. The Puritans hugged each other. They said prayers of thanks. And then they started arguing again.

Some people wanted to go to New York. It was a long way off—at least 220 miles. Others argued for staying put in Massachusetts. It was winter now. Lots of Pilgrims were very sick. A lack of vitamin-rich vegetables and fruit had given some a disease called scurvy. It makes gums bleed and teeth fall out.

Eventually the decision to stay was made. They saw that the only way to succeed was to work together. They wrote an agreement called the Mayflower Compact on Saturday, November 11, 1620. They would elect leaders and obey the laws of their new colony. They didn't want more arguments!

Only men signed the Compact. Women didn't have the same rights as men back then. A

man named John Carver was elected governor. Everyone on the *Mayflower* hoped things would turn out okay. They would work hard and do their best to make a new life—a good life—together.

Plymouth Rock

The legend goes that the Pilgrims landed on Plymouth Rock. This was a granite rock in the shallow waters of Cape Cod Bay. It weighed about twenty tons.

Did the Pilgrims really land there?

Nobody mentioned the rock in letters or records. In 1741, a man named Thomas Faunce claimed that his father said that the Rock had been the exact landing spot. That's not much proof!

Still, over the years, Plymouth Rock became a symbol of the Pilgrims' arrival in America. In 1774, some American patriots tried to move it. It broke in half! The bottom half was left in the bay. The top half was displayed in the town square. In 1820, there was a celebration at the Rock of the two-hundred-year anniversary of the *Mayflower*'s arrival.

The Rock got moved around a couple more times. In 1880, the date "1620" was carved into the top half of it. Today, both halves of Plymouth Rock are together again in Pilgrim Memorial State Park in Massachusetts. Over the years, wind and water have eroded the Rock. And people have chipped off small pieces for souvenirs. Now it's less than half of its original size.

CHAPTER 4
A New Home

The next day was Sunday, so the Pilgrims stayed on the ship to worship. On Monday, the men rowed ashore. Myles Standish, William Bradford, and fourteen other men went looking for a place to settle. The perfect spot would have trees for building homes, good hunting and fishing, some flat land for farming, and a harbor nearby.

The first thing the women did onshore was wash clothes. They built fires and heated water from a pond in big iron pots. Each Pilgrim usually owned only two outfits—one for everyday, and a special one for Sunday. After wearing the same clothes for the whole trip, everything was dirty!

Over the next few weeks, the men kept exploring. One day, they saw a group of Native Americans in the distance. The natives ran away.

The Pilgrims saw their first American deer. They found fresh water.

They also found a big basket of Indian corn stored underground. This corn was different from yellow English corn. It was bright red, orange, yellow, and blue. Once it dried out, it wouldn't rot and could be eaten through the winter. Desperate, they stole some of the corn. This meant that the Native Americans who'd harvested it would not have the corn for themselves. They might go hungry.

The Pilgrims went back later and stole the rest. On that trip, they also found empty Native American homes and some graves. They helped themselves to what they needed, taking bowls, food, and baskets. They meant to leave some beads and other goods behind in payment. But when it started to get dark, they took off without leaving anything.

This was not a good way to make friends with the native people who had been living on Cape Cod long before the Pilgrims. It's not surprising that during another trip, Native Americans attacked. They yelled war cries and shot arrows at the Pilgrims, who fired their muskets. The natives eventually retreated. As far as the Pilgrims knew, no one on either side was hurt.

On December 20, the Pilgrims finally found a good place for their settlement. The land had been cleared and farmed. Although the Pilgrims didn't know it, this had been the site of a Native American village. Everyone in the village had died from diseases brought by early European explorers and traders.

The Pilgrims named their village New Plymouth. There was a freshwater brook and a hill nearby. From the top of the hill they could watch for approaching danger.

On Christmas Day, they began building. The first building to go up was a twenty-foot-square meetinghouse. This was where the Pilgrims would make laws and have prayer meetings. But for now, only the men lived in it. The women and children stayed on the ship until new homes were ready. Some storerooms were also built. And the cannons they'd brought were placed on the hill overlooking the town.

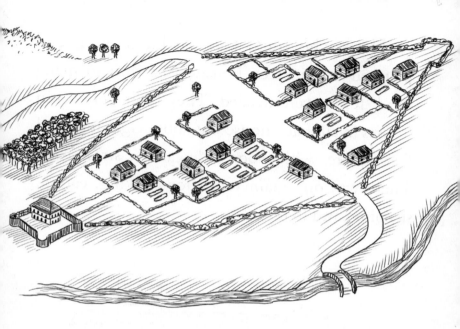

The men drew a plan of how the town might look. There would be one main street that sloped down toward the ocean. There would be a row of houses on either side of the street, and one cross street. But to make their plans come true, they had to get through the winter first.

The weather grew fierce with freezing rain and snow. The food was almost gone. It was a terrible time. Many of the Pilgrims got sick and died.

Those who could kept on building. They'd planned on nineteen houses. But with so many dead, fewer were needed. They built only seven houses in all. Each house was about eight hundred feet square, with wood sides and a straw roof. There was one main room for cooking, eating, sleeping, and living.

By the time spring came, only fifty people were still alive. Spring meant it was time to plant crops. But the Pilgrims were craftsmen—weavers, tailors, shoemakers, and printers. They didn't have the skills needed for farming in the wilderness.

Luckily, they would soon get some help.

William Bradford

In April 1621, William Bradford was elected as the second governor of Plymouth. He served for over thirty years. He was a wise, strong leader. He is important for another reason—the journal he wrote called *Of Plimoth Plantation*. (*Plimoth* is the old spelling of *Plymouth*, and the colony was called a plantation in its early years.) The journal supplied much of what we know about the Pilgrims.

Bradford began the journal in 1630. He had kept notes about the early years and saved letters and documents to help him tell the Pilgrims' story. His journal says that when they sailed from Holland in 1620, "they knew they were pilgrimes." He also wrote that in the New World, "they had now no friends to welcome them."

English explorer Captain John Smith had named northeast America "New England" on his map in 1614. This area included Massachusetts. In his journal, Governor Bradford described New England as a "wildernes, full of wild beasts and willd men." About the Pilgrims' first fall he said that they "had all things in good plenty." In 1650, he added one last page—a list of the *Mayflower* passengers.

CHAPTER 5
Making Friends

On March 16, 1621, a tall Native American man walked into Plymouth Colony. The Pilgrims worried that he planned to harm them. Instead he said, "Welcome, Englishmen!"

The Pilgrims were amazed to hear him speak English, even though he didn't speak it very well. His name was Samoset. He told them that a fisherman in Maine had taught him English. He carried a bow and two arrows. One arrow had a sharp tip. The other didn't. Although the Pilgrims didn't realize it, this was probably his way of asking a question: Had they come as enemies or as friends?

Samoset was the first Native American the Pilgrims had spoken to, so they were very interested in him. He was interested in them, too. He'd seen many European men in New England. But they were mostly traders and explorers, not settlers. And he probably hadn't seen many

English women and children before.

Samoset left. Six days later, he returned with over sixty Wampanoag. Most of the natives waited outside the settlement. They were watching for signs of trouble. Some, however, entered the colony. One was named Squanto. Another was Massasoit, the "great sachem." A sachem (say: SAY-chem) is a leader or chief.

Massasoit welcomed the Pilgrims in the Wampanoag language. They didn't understand. Squanto spoke both English and Wampanoag. He helped both sides understand each other. But was Squanto translating their words truthfully? Neither side was sure.

For instance, Squanto told Massasoit that the Pilgrims had put terrible diseases inside barrels. He said they could be used as a weapon to kill the tribe.

Why did he say this?

Squanto was trying to scare Massasoit into making friends with the colonists. Squanto wanted to stay on the Pilgrims' good side so he could gain power and become an important leader.

The Wampanoag thought maybe it was wise to join forces with these Europeans.

The Pilgrims knew they needed help. Maybe these Native Americans would supply it.

So both sides decided to be friends. Together, they made an agreement with six rules. The first rule said that the Wampanoag would not hurt the Pilgrims. Afterward, the Pilgrims gave Massasoit a gift of some English peas.

King James I of England

A depiction of the Mayflower in Plymouth Harbor

Captain Myles Standish

Governor William Bradford

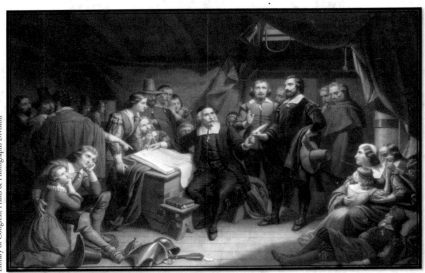

Pilgrims signing the Mayflower Compact

set doune by them done (this their condition considered) might
be as firme as any patent; and in some respects more sure.
The forme was as followeth.

In y̆ name of god Amen. We whose names are underwriten,
the loyall subjects of our dread soueraigne Lord King James
by y̆ grace of god, of great Britaine, franc, & Ireland king,
defender of y̆ faith, &c.

Haueing undertaken, for y̆ glorie of god, and aduancemente
of y̆ christian faith, and honour of our king & countrie, a voyage to
plant y̆ first colonie in y̆ Northerne parts of Virginia. doe
by these presents solemnly & mutualy in y̆ presence of god, and
one of another, couenant, & combine our selues togeather into a
ciuill body politick, for our better ordering, & preseruation & fur=
therance of y̆ ends aforesaid; and by vertue hearof to enacte,
constitute, and frame shuch just & equall Lawes, ordinances,
Acts, constitutions, & offices, from time to time, as shall be thought
most meete & conuenient for y̆ generall good of y̆ colonie: unto
which we promise all due submission and obedience. In witnes
wherof we haue hereunder subscribed our names at Cap=
Codd y̆ 11 of Nouember, in y̆ year of y̆ raigne of our soueraigne
Lord king James of England, franc, & Ireland y̆ eighteen,
and of Scotland y̆ fiftie fourth. An°: Dom. 1620.]

Governor William Bradford's transcription of the Mayflower Compact

The Granger Collection, New York

A nineteenth-century engraving of the Pilgrims
landing at Plymouth Rock in 1620

A depiction of the peace treaty between the
Pilgrims and the Wampanoag

KING PHILIP—the last of the Wampanoags. [See Page 77.]

Metacom, also known as King Philip,
the last Wampanoag chief

Samoset visiting Plymouth Colony in a nineteenth-century wood engraving

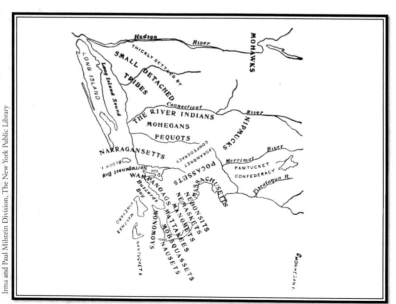

The territories of various East Coast tribes

Pilgrims on their way to church in an engraving
from a nineteenth-century painting

A depiction of the Plymouth settlement in 1623

Typical Pilgrim clothing

Plymouth town square in 1828

A cabinet that was brought over on the Mayflower

The kitchen of an original Pilgrim house

Re-creation of a Wampanoag hut at Plimouth Plantation

Thanksgiving postcard from 1914

A depiction of the Pilgrims' first Thanksgiving

Macy's Thanksgiving Day Parade in the 1920s

Squanto

Squanto was kidnapped by an English sea captain in 1614. In England, he learned to speak English. In 1618, Squanto went back to Massachusetts. By then, his village was gone. Sadly, the entire tribe had died from a disease brought over by the Europeans. Squanto was all alone—the only member of his tribe still alive.

He went to live with the Wampanoag. The chief, Massasoit, didn't really trust him. But when Squanto said that it would be a mistake to attack the Pilgrims, he listened.

Squanto stayed behind. He taught the Pilgrims how the natives hunted and fished. He showed them how to catch eels in a wooden basket. He took them into nearby forests, where plants grew that could be eaten.

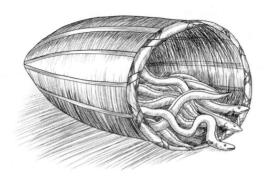

The Pilgrims had brought along barley and peas to plant. But neither grew well in the poor Plymouth soil. Squanto showed them how to plant corn and other crops instead. He told the Pilgrims to add a few dead herring fish to each mound of corn that was planted. When the fish rotted, they turned into fertilizer. Once the corn sprouted, pumpkins, squash, and beans

were planted around it. Their vines grew up the cornstalks. Their wide leaves shaded the corn from the hot sun and kept weeds down. Without Squanto's help, the Pilgrims might have all starved.

On April 5, the *Mayflower* sailed back to England. There, it sat unused and began to rot. No one is sure exactly what happened to it. Parts of it were probably sold and reused.

The Pilgrims could have returned home on the *Mayflower*, but none of them did. In fact one of the crewmen, a barrel maker named John Alden, also decided to stay in Plymouth.

The Pilgrims kept busy settling into their colony. All the children in Plymouth worked, too. They got up at sunrise and went to bed soon after sunset.

There were no faucets with running water in Pilgrim homes. Boys and girls fetched water in buckets from a nearby spring. They set the table for breakfast and helped serve it. Sometimes breakfast was hasty pudding (cornmeal cereal) or samp (corn mush).

Girls tended the cooking fire. After meals, they helped rinse or wipe the dishes clean. They helped their mothers do housework such as grinding spices, washing clothes, or sweeping the floors. They helped hang the family's straw-filled bed mattresses over the fence to air out. Girls fed the chickens with leftover food. They milked the family's cow or goat morning and afternoon.

Tending the family's garden was also girls' work. Boys fetched firewood. They fed the

livestock. When they were about seven years old, they started working in the farm fields with their fathers.

Now and then, children visited with friends. Maybe they'd play a game of marbles, which they called knickers. Or they might play all hid (hide-and-seek) or naughts and crosses (tic-tac-toe).

After supper, children studied the Bible with their fathers. They learned their ABCs, how to write their names, and some arithmetic. But that was about all the schooling children got.

Sundays were different. Working was against the rules. So was playing. There were two church services at the meetinghouse. One lasted from 8:00 a.m. till noon, and another one went from 2:00 p.m. till about 6:00 p.m. Everyone had to attend both services. It was not an easy life for a child, especially that first year.

During the spring and summer, the Pilgrims' crops grew. Their first fall harvest was good. They would have enough food for the next winter, and they would not starve. Things were looking up. They decided to celebrate.

The Wampanoag

The Wampanoag (say: wam-pa-NO-ag) lived in Massachusetts and eastern Rhode Island. They had already been there for twelve thousand years when the Pilgrims arrived in 1620.

The Wampanoag lived according to the seasons. In spring and summer, they lived along the coast. They fished and gathered grasses and wild plants. They dug clams. They grew corn, beans, and squash to eat. A dome-shaped Wampanoag home was called a *wetu* (say: WE-too). It was made of wood poles covered with cattail reeds or tree bark.

In fall and winter, they moved inland where it was warmer. They hunted bear, deer, moose, wild turkeys, and other animals for food. They used the animals' feathers and furs for clothing and blankets.

Wampanoag men did the hunting and fishing. Boys practiced with bows and arrows. Women and

girls took care of the family's *wetu*. They did the cooking, sewing, and much of the farming.

Young Wampanoag children didn't have many chores. They swam and played games. At night, the grown-ups might tell them exciting stories about the history of the tribe.

CHAPTER 6
The First Thanksgiving

People in the 1600s didn't celebrate all the holidays we do today. Instead, a day of prayer and thanksgiving would be announced whenever something special happened. It might be to celebrate winning a battle or surviving a bad winter.

They would spend most of the day in church. This kind of day was called a "thanksgiving."

But what we now call the first Thanksgiving was not like this. It was a harvest celebration. No one knows exactly when it was held, but it was sometime between mid-September and mid-November in 1621.

When Governor Bradford announced that there would be a thanksgiving, he was not trying to create an important holiday. The colony was simply going to celebrate the end of a good harvest. The Pilgrims had no idea it would become a national holiday in a country called the United States.

Artists have painted pictures showing the Pilgrim feast outdoors at a long table covered in white linen. They did eat outdoors and may have brought some furniture outside, including tables. But they didn't all sit at one long table. They probably stood or squatted. Or they sat on benches, chairs, barrels, or the ground.

Children, women, and servants probably brought out food. Then everyone helped themselves.

The best food was served to the most important people. Their plates and bowls were made either of a metal called pewter or of wood. They didn't have forks, only knives and spoons. Mostly they ate with their fingers or ate bites of food speared on the tip of a knife. They wore big napkins tucked around their necks to wipe their hands and mouths.

There's a legend that the Pilgrims invited the Wampanoag to their feast. Maybe they did; maybe they didn't. Maybe this is the way things went: The Pilgrims were shooting off their muskets for fun. Some Wampanoag heard the noise. Was there going to be an attack? They came to find out. When they saw that the Pilgrims were only having fun, they joined in.

Did the Pilgrims invite them to stay? Maybe. The Pilgrims were probably in a good mood—a sharing mood.

All of the Pilgrims were likely to have attended this first Thanksgiving. There were about ninety Wampanoag, including Massasoit and Squanto.

The Wampanoag went out and hunted five deer to add to the feast. The Pilgrims also cooked and ate geese and ducks. They probably had wild turkey and foods such as

corn, pumpkin, squash, peas, and beans.

There also might have been walnuts, chestnuts, plums, quail, pigeons, or partridges. And possibly seafood, including bass and cod.

There was no cranberry sauce or pumpkin pie. They probably ate berries for dessert.

And maybe they drank beer made from barley. Back then, people were afraid of drinking water.

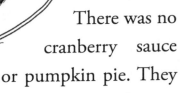

They didn't have water systems in cities and towns, so the water often was dirty.

All around them, the trees were turning bright colors. Back home in England, the leaf colors were not so bright. The first fall in New England must have been a beautiful sight.

Edward Winslow's Letter

A Pilgrim named Edward Winslow was at the first Thanksgiving. He described it like this in a letter written on December 12, 1621:

"Our harvest being gotten in, our governor [William Bradford] sent four men on fowling, that so we might after a special manner rejoice together after we had gathered the fruits of our labors. They four in one day killed as much fowl, as with a little help beside, served the company almost a week. At which time amongst other recreations, we exercised our arms, many of the Indians coming amongst us, and amongst the rest their greatest king Massasoit, with some ninety men, whom for three days we entertained and feasted, and they went out and killed five deer, which they brought to the Plantation and bestowed on our governor, and upon the captain [Myles Standish] and others."

CHAPTER 7
Fun and Games

The Pilgrims and Native Americans did more than eat and chat for those three days in 1621. The Pilgrims were relaxing for a change. They wanted some fun!

Some of the men marched in a parade. They probably showed off their musket-shooting skills by doing target practice.

They probably played simple games. Pilgrims might have shown the Wampanoag games called lummelen (keep-away) or draughts (checkers). They might've played blindman's bluff.

The Wampanoag might've shown the Pilgrims how to play a toss-and-catch game. The player would hold a stick with string tied to a ring made of twisted vine. Flipping the ring in the air, the player would try to catch it on the pointed end of the stick. This kind of game helped with hand-eye coordination and made them better hunters.

There may have been lots of footraces. The Wampanoag were fast runners. They may have sung native songs and performed native dances for the Pilgrims.

Paintings of the first Thanksgiving often show the Pilgrims wearing black clothes and hats, and shoes with buckles. They didn't really dress like this. Their everyday clothes were often brown or red, because those were easy dye colors to make. Sometimes they were green or blue.

The Pilgrims and the Wampanoag were very different. They spoke different languages. They lived in different kinds of houses. Neither side completely understood or trusted the other. By celebrating together, they got to know each other better. Maybe they learned that they had more in common than it first seemed.

But sadly, their friendships didn't last forever.

How the Pilgrims Dressed

COIF

WAISTCOAT

POCKET

PETTICOATS

COLLAR

DOUBLET

SMOCK

APRON

STOCKINGS

FLOPPY HAT

LONG-SLEEVE SHIRT

BREECHES

LEATHER SHOES

How the Wampanoag Dressed

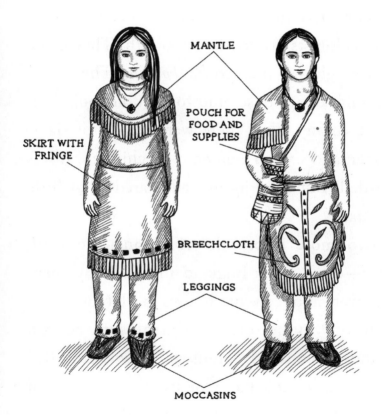

MANTLE

POUCH FOR FOOD AND SUPPLIES

SKIRT WITH FRINGE

BREECHCLOTH

LEGGINGS

MOCCASINS

CHAPTER 8
Trouble

Soon after the first Thanksgiving, thirty-five more colonists arrived in Plymouth. They came on an English ship called the *Fortune*. There were still only seven houses and four public buildings in the colony. Now there were a total of sixty-six men and sixteen women, plus children. It was crowded! But the Pilgrims all shared what little they had.

Two more ships—the *Anne* and the *Little James*—came from England in 1623. By then, there were about twenty houses in Plymouth.

In 1630, a group of seventeen ships arrived with around a thousand colonists. They established the Massachusetts Bay Colony. It was north of Plymouth near where Boston is today.

More settlers meant even more building. More trees were cut down to make more houses. The settlers were taking over the areas where the Wampanoag had always farmed, fished, and hunted. The Pilgrims' animals were trampling the natives' cornfields.

The Pilgrims and other colonists saw New England as an empty wilderness. When they arrived, there were no houses, roads, or stores like they were used to in Europe. To them, Native

Americans were savages because they lived in a different way. The Pilgrims believed they were special and that God wanted them to claim the land in America for their own.

The Wampanoag had their own religion. They believed there were spirits in the rivers and forests around them. Land—all of nature—didn't belong to anyone. So when colonists made deals to buy land, it didn't make sense to the Native Americans. They thought they would still be able to farm, hunt, and fish on the land after they sold it. They were angry when the colonists wouldn't let them. These problems would end in war between the colonists and Native Americans.

William Bradford and Massasoit both died in the 1650s. These strong leaders had helped keep the peace. Massasoit's sons, Wamsutta and Metacom, kept their father's promises at first. But they were getting angry. Then something terrible happened.

In 1662, the Pilgrims captured Wamsutta. At Plymouth, he got sick and died. Why had they done such a thing? The Wampanoag were furious.

Metacom, who was also called King Philip, became the Wampanoag leader. He thought that to survive, his people had to drive the Pilgrims away. In 1675, he led attacks against English settlements all around New England. The English settlers attacked the Wampanoag in return.

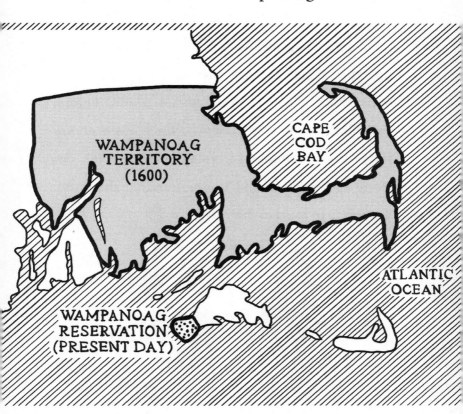

WAMPANOAG
TERRITORY
(1600)

CAPE
COD
BAY

ATLANTIC
OCEAN

WAMPANOAG
RESERVATION
(PRESENT DAY)

This was called King Philip's War. Many were killed on both sides. A year later, most of the Native American villages had been destroyed.

What Happened to the Wampanoag?

Wampanoag means "people of the east." They got the name because they lived in southeast Massachusetts and eastern Rhode Island. Before the Pilgrims came to America, there were about sixty-seven Wampanoag villages. Altogether, as many as fifty thousand to one hundred thousand Wampanoag lived in the villages.

From 1616 to 1618, thousands of them died from diseases Europeans had brought with them. More died later in battles with the colonists who were taking over their land. The tribe was dying out.

After King Philip's War, English settlers sold some of the natives into slavery in the Caribbean islands. Others became servants to New England colonists. The Wampanoag lost their freedom, their families, and their way of life.

By the 1800s, many Wampanoag were speaking English and wearing English-style clothes. Their native language was in danger of being forgotten. Old documents such as a 1650s Bible translated into Wampanoag have helped preserve their language. Other documents and stories passed down from their ancestors show the way they lived long ago.

There are about five thousand Wampanoag now. Most live in Massachusetts.

CHAPTER 9
A Thanksgiving Holiday

In December 1769, some men in Plymouth decided to honor the Pilgrims for the hardships they had suffered to come to America. They shot a cannon, gave speeches, and had a feast.

Twenty years later, the first US president, George Washington, tried to make Thanksgiving a national holiday. He didn't succeed. But in 1820—two hundred years after the Pilgrims landed in Massachusetts—there was another celebration in Plymouth to honor them. A politician named Daniel Webster made a famous speech. He called them America's "Pilgrim Fathers."

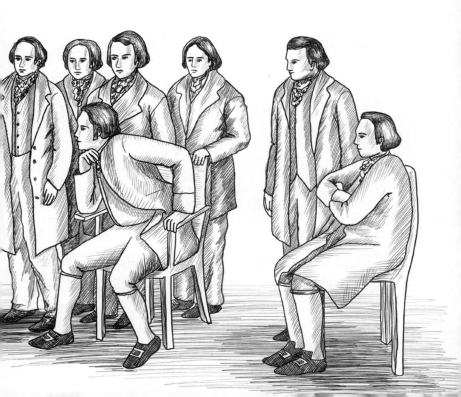

From then on, interest in the Pilgrims slowly grew all over the United States. Artists painted pictures of the Pilgrims and their first Thanksgiving. Many of the paintings were not accurate. The Pilgrims looked solemn. They were dressed in black and were in the center of the paintings, with only a few Native Americans around the edges.

INACCURATE PAINTING OF THANKSGIVING

Soon, many of the states were celebrating Thanksgiving, but on whatever day that suited them. Then along came a woman named Sarah Hale. She was determined that everyone in the United States should celebrate Thanksgiving on the exact same day, just like one big, united family. She wanted to make it a real national holiday.

In 1837, Hale was the editor of a popular magazine for women called *Godey's Lady's Book*. In it, she suggested ideas for Thanksgiving foods, games, and decorations. She wrote thousands of letters to politicians asking for a national Thanksgiving holiday. Her readers did, too.

Hale even wrote to the president of the United States, Zachary Taylor. She asked for a national Thanksgiving holiday. He didn't do anything.

Every time a new president was elected, Sarah wrote again. She asked Millard Fillmore, Franklin Pierce, and James Buchanan. The answers she got were all the same: no.

The Civil War began in the United States in 1861. The Northern states fought against the Southern states. It was a terrible time for the whole country. Abraham Lincoln was president.

Hale told him that a national Thanksgiving Day was more important than ever. It might not stop the war. But it would bring people together. It would remind them that the United States was one big family of states.

President Lincoln agreed!

In 1863, he declared Thanksgiving a national holiday. After that, Thanksgiving was celebrated every year on the fourth Thursday of November.

In 1939, President Franklin Roosevelt tried changing the date to the third Thursday in November. This was to help businesses that were struggling during the years of the Great Depression. Christmas shopping began the day after Thanksgiving. With more days to shop, maybe people would buy more, and businesses would do better. This didn't work. And so in 1941, a law was passed. Thanksgiving would always be on the fourth Thursday in November.

That's the way it's been ever since.

Sarah Hale

Sarah Hale was born in New Hampshire in 1788. Back then, girls learned how to cook, sew, and clean house. But her mother also taught her how to read and write. When she grew up, she became a teacher. One day a lamb followed one of her students to school. She wrote a nursery rhyme about it called "Mary Had a Little Lamb." It's still famous today!

Later, she got married and had five children. When her husband died, she got a job making hats. But she wanted to be an author. At thirty-nine, she published a novel called *Northwood*. It was a hit, which helped her get a job as the editor of the *Ladies' Magazine* in 1827. This was a big deal. No other woman in America had ever been a magazine editor.

Her magazine published the stories of great authors like Edgar Allan Poe, Charles Dickens, and

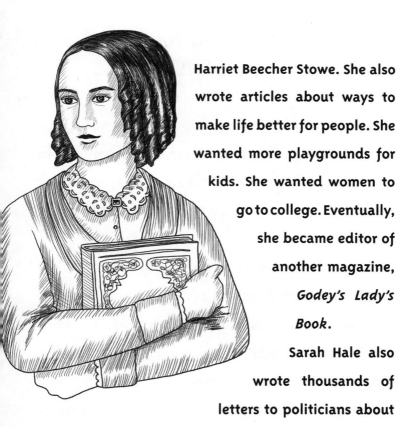

Harriet Beecher Stowe. She also wrote articles about ways to make life better for people. She wanted more playgrounds for kids. She wanted women to go to college. Eventually, she became editor of another magazine, *Godey's Lady's Book.*

Sarah Hale also wrote thousands of letters to politicians about Thanksgiving. Without her, there might not be a national Thanksgiving holiday in the United States!

CHAPTER 10
Thanksgiving Today

Many of our Thanksgiving holiday traditions are based on the Pilgrims' first Thanksgiving in 1621. Like the Pilgrims, we take time to remember the good things in our lives and be thankful for them.

Thanksgiving is a time for sharing. For example, some people collect food to donate to people who don't have enough to eat. Families get together and share a big meal. Aunts, uncles, grandparents, great-grandparents, parents, and children gather. Like the Pilgrims, many families pray together on Thanksgiving.

They eat many of the same foods the Pilgrims and Native Americans shared. And some that the Pilgrims and Native Americans never heard of.

Often Thanksgiving decorations of fall leaves or cornstalks are put on the table.

The Thanksgiving practice of playing games has continued. Many people watch football games. The first football game on Thanksgiving Day was in the 1870s. In the 1890s, the game between two college teams—Princeton and Yale—drew huge crowds. Today thousands of college and high-school football games are played on Thanksgiving Day.

Turkey Facts

Nowadays, Thanksgiving turkeys are raised on farms. They weigh twice as much as wild turkeys. Wild turkeys live in the forests of North America and were the kind the Pilgrims ate. Wild turkeys can fly, but farm turkeys can't.

FARM TURKEY

WILD TURKEY

Only male turkeys make a *gobble* sound. Female turkeys make a *click* sound.

Benjamin Franklin wanted the turkey to be the national bird of the United States. In 1782, the bald eagle was chosen instead.

About forty-six million turkeys are eaten in the United States on Thanksgiving.

The National Turkey Federation gives the president of the United States a live turkey during a ceremony each year. It is not eaten. Sometimes the turkeys are sent to Mount Vernon to live. That was George Washington's home. Some of the turkeys have even been part of the Disneyland Thanksgiving Parade in California.

The Pilgrims marched in a parade with their muskets. Today there are still Thanksgiving parades. The most famous parade takes place in New York City and is run by Macy's department store. The first Macy's Thanksgiving Day Parade was in 1924. There were decorated floats, musical bands, and real elephants, bears, and camels from the Central Park Zoo. The parade went from 145th Street in Harlem to the Macy's store on 34th Street.

By 1927, the zoo animals had been replaced by big animal-shaped balloons filled with helium. In 1929, the balloons were released at the end of the parade and allowed to float away. Whoever eventually found a balloon won a gift from Macy's. Gathering to watch parades is now a Thanksgiving tradition in many families.

Today, you can visit Plimoth Plantation. It is an outdoor living-history museum that re-creates the Pilgrims' village. It looks like Plymouth probably did in 1627. That's seven years after the Pilgrims arrived there on the *Mayflower*. You can walk through the village. The houses, beds, furniture, gardens, animals, and food you'll see are all like what the Pilgrims had. It's as if you have traveled back in time!

You'll get to see and talk to people who dress like the Pilgrims did in 1627. They are not actual Pilgrims, but they do act and speak like Pilgrims. You can ask them questions. They know a lot about how the Pilgrims lived. But if you ask them about anything modern, like computers or TV, they will pretend they don't know what you're talking about.

You can go into many of the houses in the village. You might see Pilgrims cooking or eating dinner. You might see them gardening, playing

draughts, mending clothes, repairing a roof, or building a fire. You can ask them about how their homes were built and what they grow in their small gardens. (An herb called sage was mixed with salt to make toothpaste in Pilgrim times!)

You can also visit the fort, where Pilgrim guards

watched over the town. They kept an eye out for enemies and accidental fires. You might see how a musket is loaded and fired.

Near Plimoth Plantation, you can also visit a re-created Wampanoag homesite. It's located on the bank of the Eel River. This area was used by

the Wampanoag for planting and fishing for over a thousand years. The Wampanoag you'll meet are all descendants from the real Wampanoag or from other Native American nations. They wear historically accurate clothes. Most are made of deerskin.

You'll see how the Wampanoag lived in the spring and fall of 1627. You might see them fish, plant crops, and gather berries. Or weave baskets or cook.

You might see natives using fire to hollow out a tree trunk. They are making a *mishoon*. That's the Wampanoag word for "boat."

The people you meet at the Wampanoag Homesite do not pretend to live in Pilgrim times. But they can tell you about Wampanoag history and culture. They might invite you inside the mat-covered *wetu*. Or into a bark-covered longhouse called a *nush wetu* with several fire pits inside.

They might show you how to play hubbub. That's an old Native American game played using five fruit pits or coin-shaped bits of bone. One side of each pit is painted. The other side is blank. Players take turns tossing the pits into a bowl or shaking the bowl. The object is to get the pits to land painted side up.

The *Mayflower II* is also part of Plimoth Plantation. The ship is an actual-size copy of the original *Mayflower*. You can see the ship's sails and oak timbers. Aboard the ship, you'll see the kinds of equipment sailors used, such as horn lanterns and hand-colored maps. You might be surprised by how small the ship feels when you're on board. It's hard to imagine all the Pilgrims living in the cramped tween decks for ten weeks. The captain's cabin is small, but it looks more comfortable than where the sailors slept!

Plimoth Plantation is located near the site of the Pilgrims' actual village. The address is 137 Warren Avenue in Plymouth, Massachusetts. That's about a one-hour drive from Boston, Massachusetts, or from Providence, Rhode Island.

Today, Plymouth is still one of the most important landmarks in the United States. The Pilgrims found religious freedom there. Even when trouble and death came their way, the Pilgrims of Plymouth did not give up. Their determination and spirit made other Americans proud. Their story and the legend of their first Thanksgiving inspired our own Thanksgiving holiday!

Timeline of the First Thanksgiving

1607	The first English colony in North America is founded in Jamestown
1608	John Smith becomes the leader of the Jamestown settlement
1620	The Pilgrims sail to America from England on a ship called the *Mayflower*
	The Pilgrims write the Mayflower Compact, an agreement detailing the laws they would follow
1621	In Plymouth, Massachusetts, the Pilgrims celebrate a harvest feast that many consider to be the first Thanksgiving
1777	The first Thanksgiving in the newly established United States of America takes place, with all thirteen colonies celebrating
1789	George Washington, America's first president, declares November 26 to be a day for thanksgiving and prayer across the nation
1846	An editor named Sarah Hale begins a campaign to set the last Thursday in November as the national Thanksgiving Day
1863	Abraham Lincoln issues a proclamation making a national day of thanksgiving an annual tradition
1924	The first annual Macy's Thanksgiving Day Parade is held in New York City

Timeline of the World

The first modern novel, Miguel de Cervantes's — 1605
Don Quixote de la Mancha, is published

Galileo Galilei spots Jupiter's moons through his telescope — 1610

King James version of the Bible published in England — 1611

William Shakespeare dies — 1616

The Thirty Years' War, in which Protestants — 1618
fought against Catholic control, begins

Construction begins for the Taj Mahal in India — 1632

English Civil War begins — 1642

End of the Ming dynasty in China — 1644

Bubonic plague kills at least 75,000 people in London — 1665

England, Wales, and Scotland join — 1707
together to form Great Britain

Stamp Act passed, taxing paper documents in the colonies — 1765

Quartering Act passed, requiring colonists
to house and feed British soldiers

Fourteen-year-old Marie Antoinette — 1770
arrives at the French court

The Boston Tea Party occurs on the night of December 16 — 1773

The Continental Congress authorizes — 1776
the Declaration of Independence

The Revolutionary War ends with America's independence — 1783

Bibliography

*Books for young readers

*Anderson, Laurie Halse. *Thank You, Sarah!: The Woman Who Saved Thanksgiving*. New York: Simon & Schuster Books For Young Readers, 2002.

*Erickson, Paul. *Daily Life in the Pilgrim Colony 1636*. New York: Clarion Books, 2001.

*Grace, Catherine O'Neill and Margaret M. Bruchac. *1621: A New Look at Thanksgiving*. Washington, DC: National Geographic Children's Books, 2001.

Hillstrom, Laurie C. *The Thanksgiving Book*. Detroit: Omnigraphics, 2007.

*Landau, Elaine. *Celebrate the First Thanksgiving with Elaine Landau*. New Jersey: Enslow Publishers, 2006.

*MacMillan, Dianne M. *Thanksgiving Day*. New Jersey: Enslow Publishers, 1997.

*McGovern, Ann. . . . *If You Sailed on the Mayflower in 1620*. New York: Scholastic, 1969.

*Osborne, Mary Pope and Natalie Pope Boyce. *Pilgrims: A Nonfiction Companion to Magic Tree House #27: Thanksgiving on Thursday*. New York: Random House Children's Books, 2005.

*Philbrick, Nathaniel. *The Mayflower and the Pilgrims' New World*. New York: G. P. Putnam's Sons, 2008.

*Plimoth Plantation. ***Mayflower 1620: A New Look at a Pilgrim Voyage***. Washington, DC: National Geographic Children's Books, 2003.

*Waters, Kate. ***Tapenum's Day: A Wampanoag Indian Boy in Pilgrim Times***. New York: Scholastic, 1996.